GIVETH AND TAKETH

Rota

Wild Pressed Books

First Edition.

This book is a work of non-fiction.

The publisher has no control over, and is not responsible for, any third party websites or their contents.

Giveth and Taketh © 2020 by Rota.

Original cover photograph by Ben Ostrower on Unsplash

Cover Design by Tracey Scott-Townsend

ISBN: 9781916489691

Contact the author via twitter: @TheMCRota

English language edition.

Published by Wild Pressed Books: 2020

Wild Pressed Books, UK Business Reg. No. 09550738

http://www.wildpressedbooks.com

"Rota has an unrivaled ability to weave the political and the personal into lyric, to loose it with piercing wit, to present each poem as a volley of arrows. Better yet the poems amalgamate to form a Golem to safeguard the most precious thing; place – yes location location location, but moreso place of self within the complexities of race, religion and family. Giveth and Taketh is trenchant, satirical, and just plain smart!"
– Jay Ward, Individual World Poetry Slam Champion 2020

"Rota's Giveth and Taketh is a cheeky look at what it's like to be an invisible Jew noticed only in times of convenience. When it is convenient to hate them, when it is convenient to blame them, when it is convenient to gain from them. This collection is not only chock full of cohesive political, biblical, and pop culture references, but if you look closely, you can detect self-deprecating moxie and a sly middle finger. "
– Lannie Stabile, author of Little Masticated Darlings

"Rota possesses that seemingly mystical jewish quality of managing to make the tragic and banal beautiful and comic. He perfectly captures the perpetual state of betweenness—White or other, inside or out, safe or imperiled, faith or people—that defines American Jewishness today."
– Jamie Moshin, Professor of Communications and Media/Judaic Studies, University of Michigan

"Rota's work is so accessible as it illustrates his own great events within the usual, everyday, even mundane. Rota's vulnerability seems to parallel our own but his conversational expression of it leans toward parable."
– Billy Tuggle, author of Incantation and four-time Chicago poetry Grand Slam Champion

Dedicated to my family - Mom, Dad, Sara, Aaron, and Kira - for making Judaism a source of good conversation and good food.

I'm not going to claim that my grandparents can see this from heaven or something because that doesn't feel very Jewish, but I can say that I think Nana Murkie, Papa Mel, Nana Dee, and Papa Sam would have been particularly proud of this book while also lovingly disagreeing with parts of it.

I love you all very much.

"'It's not a pretty world, Papa.'
'I've noticed,' my father said softly."
— *Chaim Potok, My Name Is Asher Lev*

GIVETH AND TAKETH

Contents

To the man at the waspy dinner party who told me I'd go to Hell

(if I didn't embrace Jesus)

As if heat is punishment to a diaspora teeming with grandparents who retire to Southern Florida. Who left the desert to flee from Krakow to Brooklyn to Boca Raton just to bask in the viscous summer air and describe 76 degrees as "jacket weather." Hell! Where it's never too cold for shuffleboard. Hell! Where we can always have a good schvitz. It's like a sauna down here and the ovens can't kill us. This eternal summer camp. This tropical birthright. Maybe I'll meet a nice Jewish girl.

My Nana will be so damned proud.

Jew Boy White Boy

After Angel Nafis and Jon Sands

Jew boy white boy
For now
Jew boy born in 1981 Chicagoland
Jew boy born white boy

1971 Jew boys white boys
1961 Jew boys white boys
1951 Jew boys Jew boys
1941 Jew boys dead boys
1931 Jew boys white boys

2019 Jew boy write Jew boy
Oppression poem. Audience peeved
Because Jew boy
White boy

Jew boy white guilt
Jew boy Black Lives Matter rally
Jew boy pro-Palestine rally
But still take free trip to Israel
Jew boy pray at Wailing Wall
Not sure who he's praying to
Jew boy can't spell G-d
Jew boy atheist
And doesn't understand why that's so confusing
Jew boy care more about Drake being Jewish
Than God being Jewish

1471 Jew boy European boy
1481 Jew boy European boy
1491 Jew boy Jew boy
1492 Jew boy ash

Jew boy lights the candles
But doesn't know the prayers
Jew boy atheist but still seek Jewish girl
Jew boy and Jew girl walk in seven circles
Under godless chupah
Raise holy children
In godless house
Jew boy Jew girl
Have Jew boy

Jew boy white boy
Jew boy white boy
White boy Jew boy
White boy forget he Jew boy

For now

We Again Go Unmentioned

The poet lists the kinds of bodies endangered
by this flailing hate crime of a president
and we again go unmentioned even just days after
the bullets made their own minion in a Pittsburgh synagogue
and again our ancestors' stories of hiding and flight are a
rhetorical flourish

and again the Hebrew fades from the graveyards

and again the history books are redacted in plain white ink

and again they speak of Nazis without speaking of Jews

and again the fires in Boston

and again the fires in London

and again resisting erasure is "oppression Olympics"

and again our pink stars are too violent for the Women's
March

and again our rainbow stars are too imperial for Pride

and again the Right plays puppeteer

and again the Left grows suspicious

and again we are reminded that the fate of a diaspora is to
wander

From the Perspective of Chanukah

I am the American dream personified.
The essence of the self-made man.
Most people think I am the most important Jewish holiday.
I am not even in the Bible,
only tucked into the Apocrypha like a deleted scene,
yet look at me alongside these others no one has heard of:
Shemini Atzeret, Simchat Torah, Tu B'Shvat.
When was the last time you saw a Hallmark card for Yom
    Kippur?
Yom Kippur is about repentance and fasting.
Call it a High Holiday all you want,
but guilt and hunger don't sell.

I sell.

I started from the bottom.
Drake started a child star. I started with nothing.
Yet here I am—
8 days of Xbox games, of slow dancing with Geoffrey the Toys
    R Us giraffe.
I am so popular, Middle America Walmarts say *Happy
    Holidays* on Christmas because of me,
while I ride the season like a racehorse yelling *location location
    location*
as Rosh Hashanah looks on longingly from autumn.
Sure, if I was a better man I might share the limelight
with these holier days devoted to family and forgiveness,
but this is capitalism. My value is in your hands,
and every year you choose me, against all odds.
I am not some feel-good Fourth of July.

Yay! We're free from England!
We don't have to wear those fucking wigs anymore!

My tale is one of right-wing Hebrews
gaining victory to better oppress moderate Jews.
But still, everyone loves me. I've got lunch boxes and shit.
I don't need that pansy-ass Thanksgiving's McGraw-Hill
   textbook consultants
to knit a quilt from my broken glass narrative.
I succeed, without help. I don't need help.

I was born on Christmas.
Jesus wasn't even born on Christmas.

So take it from me, Jewish High Holidays,
with your three-hour liturgies
and introspective world peace bullshit,
Sukkot with your dated wishes for a plentiful harvest.
What was your miracle, Pesach? Swarms of locusts? Stone
   tablets?
I'm sure those just fly off the shelf.
Oil was my miracle! That's that shit we go to war for.
Halliburton doesn't hire mercenaries to capture unleavened
   bread.
Your archaic rituals are fossils.
I am the petroleum meniscus rising above them.
Just watch my dreidel spin. Watch the winner
snatch up the pot. And why shouldn't he?

He earned it.

Ronald Reagan Was an Idiot (and other observations about my birth year)

I was born late.
I could give any number of reasons I wanted to stay put.
Every birth is a bad hair day for the baby.
The star of *Bedtime for Bonzo* had been
elected to lead us through the Cold War. Maybe I wanted
to stick it out until Christmas.
Jews born on Christmas wind up a pretty big deal sometimes.
Plus, the world can be a scary place.
My mom saw *The Shining* while I was in utero.
In my cocoon it must have sounded like a
      whisper wielding an ax.

There's nothing more sinister than a secret.
How it makes the ears twitch like a dog barking
at an earthquake that's not yet shook. I wonder if
      I mouthed *Here's Johnny* as I burst into the world.

I was born into the winter of 1981
to a twenty-below wind-chill.
In other words, I was born into a world
where we still had winter.
They don't tell children their plans to keep us warm,
to poison the air until the snow melts
so the mosquitos can fly their violent love
      anywhere they wish.

When I was born, the President was an idiot.
Chalking this up to dementia is an insult to dementia.

But when you're born into the right skin,
to parents who can tell the schools how to pray,
you can go from shitty actor to shitty governor
to shitty president and still die to become the deity
so many pray to when they're laying
      awake at night fearing demographic shifts.

There's nothing more sinister than a secret we all know
but pretend to forget.
How every newborn is the property of their ancestors' access
   to wheat.
How the cradle can be the grave.
How the grave can be a magic phone booth
that makes men perfect,
      redacts our flaws like a designer toupee.

Every funeral is a good hair day for the dead.
Even the most desperate comb-over appears at peace.
But the ice is thawing.
The seas are rising.
And the warm flooding earth
      doesn't preserve anything.

Christianity Dis Track

You're so Christian
you eat everything bagels

You're so Christian
you have a thinning beard

You're so Christian
you forgot Jesus wasn't

You're so Christian
your name is Christian

You're so Christian
#TheMayflower

You're so Christian
you're from Maine

You're so Christian
you tried to save a wretch like me

You're so Christian
you pretend death isn't sad

so these obsequies are littered
with praise hymns and descriptions of paradise.
As if God is good today.
As if we don't need to mourn
because we'll see Mary again soon.
As if you can find hope here.
Maybe I'm jealous

you're so Christian
you can find hope here.

Us Jews are a
dust to dust people.

Maybe I'm jealous you pray to a god
who can make things rise

While Contemplating *School Ties* in a DC Airport without Air Conditioning

The tram in the Ronald Reagan National Airport is hotter than
the shower scene in School Ties, where we can be forgiven
for missing the swastika on the wall
because, in the foreground,
Matt Damon and Chris O'Donnell are both topless,
as if to say *this is how dirty Nazis get clean.*
(Which, of course, brings me to
the fantasy shared by all self-respecting Jewish men
of being portrayed by a young and glistening Brendan Fraser
while facing harassment from a strapping gaggle of sexy neo-
    fascists.)

Meanwhile, I swipe through my bad news machine
and learn the President just tweeted
that Rashida Tlaib should go back to her native land.
Which confirms what we already knew
    That the motherfucker is an uglier version of his KKK
        father;
    That the whipping branch never falls far from the poplar
        tree;
And/or that the Commander in Chief of the American military
    thinks Detroit is a country.

The point is: it's hard to say why I'm sweating.

Political outrage? The fact that this train feels like it must
have travelled through the literal fires of hell to get to the
Ronald Reagan Washington National Airport baggage claim?
Global warming? The District's transformation from a balmy

swamp to a blazing Tiki torch?

The anxious realization all of these explanations are basically
saying the same thing?
> That America is straddling the thinning moat between
> furnace and gas chamber.
> That amidst enough hot air a dog whistle starts to sound
> like a fire alarm.
> That it's hard not to wonder where we'll start routing our
> trains.

No one wins in this heat. We're all stuck here and sweltering.
The lucky ones get clean water to wash off the sweat.
The lucky ones get trains where the doors open.
The President tells us we'll be safe as long as we stick with
him,

tries to play anti-Semitism like a clarinet but sounds like a
kazoo.
Claims the Congresswoman hates us because her people are
from the desert.
But so are mine.
And between the Muslim legislator from Detroit
and the man wearing Richard Spencer's back hair as a toupee,
it gets pretty easy to figure who's the fellow religious minority
and who's the prep school Nazi. So maybe it's not the heat.

Heat is only Hell to the deserving.
Heat is only Hell to those with no escape.

Maybe it's not the heat. Maybe it's the driver.
Maybe it's time to flood the cockpit. Jump the track.
And burn everything down.

L'dor Vador

"Overall, [the study indicated that] Jews had a higher period
prevalence of DSMIII major depression than ... all non-Jews
combined."

- Itzhak Levav, M.D., et al., Journal of American Psychology

Coming from a people whose god mostly appears
as a burning plant or a violent reprimand

it's no wonder
my internal monologue is fucked.

This is the heritage we dance around
at the dinner table. The sadness born of survival.
L'dor vador - from generation to generation.

Our stomachs full but restless
all the same. Perhaps this is the price paid
for a strangely persistent gene pool

or penance for some original sin.
Not our mother eating an apple.
Not the construction of a calf in the desert.

But more likely our patriarch's willingness to sacrifice
his boy. Strap him to the altar and bring down the blade
until an angel stayed his obedient butchery.

And thereafter, God made us love His creations so deeply
that we would disobey His word to protect them.
But that love too grew restless, full but panicked,
guided only by our own tremblings –

My mother praying for my safety
because I took out the car. My father waking
every hour to make sure he locked the door.

The dedication of our holiest days
to repentance

The burdensome knowledge of what we might become
were there only blades and no angels.

Winter

Precious in the sight of the Lord is the death of his faithful servants.
- *Psalms 116:15*

I

Uncle Selwyn's makes 4 funerals this winter. Service was touching but dragged. Good lox but stale bagels at the shivah. Good to see my cousins. Hard to see them cry. Good dark chocolate pretzels.

II

G-d giveth and
taketh

Give nephew
Take grandpa

Give cancer
Take uncle

Take loved ones
Give bereavement days

III

Aunt June's Funeral. Third this Winter. Graveside Service. Cold but Pleasant.
No Tears.No Eulogy. Brief Shivah. Few Snacks.

IV

g-d

lonely

glutton

prayer

littered

Receipt

giveth

nothing

back

Midrash

*In the book of Genesis, God commands Abraham to ascend
Mount Moriah and offer his son Isaac as a sacrifice.
Abraham obeys God without question. In this telling of the
story, the part of Abraham will be played by Muriel
Levinson, my Jewish grandmother.*

You want me to sacrifice   my boy?
        But we're having dinner this Wednesday.
        Why would I do
            such a thing?

        You want to test my faith?
           I don't need faith.
                I have a family

        that goes back longer than You do

until before we invented You
        spelled Your name unpronounceable
            myth made Your golden calves
        and Your floods
            and Your six million thankless Jobs

But I suppose You work in "mysterious ways."
        At my age, I don't need mysterious ways.
        I enjoy the holidays

and we don't need You for those anymore
thank You very much.

            Wait a minute!

        Is something wrong?
Have You eaten?
        Let me make You
some food.

Like I always tell the kids,
> it's good to be hungry
> but don't get hungry
for the wrong things.

Not that it's any of my business,
> but I think You should eat something.

Or maybe lie down.
> Are You tired?
I'm worried about you.
You seem tired
> Why would You be so tired?
It seems like You've been sleeping for a long time

From the protest

and maybe tonight our words will form a Golem and it will render our enemies small and we'll awaken God and He'll get back to all that smiting but with better aim this time and our boots will erode this whole city until everything on top bleeds into a desolate landslide that lasts only as long as this tide and the Kingdom of God will have meaning and Revelations will have meaning and it will be exactly the meaning we need it to have or maybe our prayers are just bellowed hopes that never reach anyone capable of saving the harvest or waking the dead because maybe the Red Sea didn't part from the heavens but from the tremors of enough stamping feet and this is all we are, the loving embrace of an earthquake to its own shockwave, and we are the Golem, protecting ourselves from all of the eyes that only view us as mud.

Acknowledgements

Thank you to the following publications for giving a home to the following pieces included in this collection:

Entropy and Alternating Current - *Ronald Reagan Was an Idiot (and other observations about my birth year)*

FreezeRay Poetry - *From the Perspective of Chanukah*

Paragon Press - *To the man as the waspy dinner party who told me I would go to hell*

Thoughtcrime Press - *Jew Boy, White Boy & From the protest*

Ramblings over music available at
www.soundcloud.com/mcrota

Also a huge shout for so, so many things to the MMPR collective, #AwkwardJews, Rogue Tendency, Interfaith Poets, Ann Arbor, Champaign, and Chicago.